PRINCIPLES
AND
EFFICACY
OF THE
RULE OF LAW

PRINCIPLES AND EFFICACY OF THE RULE OF LAW

Dr. Michael Dassama

To order additional copies of this book, contact:
Xlibris
UK TFN: 0800 0148620 (Toll Free inside the UK)
UK Local: (02) 0369 56328 (+44 20 3695 6328 from outside the UK)
www.Xlibrispublishing.co.uk
Orders@Xlibrispublishing.co.uk
845173

CONTENTS

INTRODUCTION

The term Rule of Law, is everyday usage which is very common amongst both intellectuals and none intellectual. It is a term that is user friendly and magnetically attractive within national and international law. It is the bed-rock of our civil liberty and democratic values within the concept of constitutional and moral ethos. It depicts who we are as humans in terms of rights, privileges, freedom and protection and safe guards against tyranny, despotism, dictatorship constitutional abuse of power in the bid to protect, preserved and codified the basic fundamental principles of Human Rights.

No civilised society of our human world can be recognised in the absence of the application and the fair interpretation of the Rule of Law as enshrined in respective geo- political constitutions. It is a common adage that God made man and man in turn creates the kind of society for habitation in which rules and regulations are structurally put in place for peaceful and decent existence where, it is expected of us, to exist side by side with each other, respecting our divergent moral social values.

Over the years, social scientists and legal experts have struggled to put forward, theories that tend to attempt subtle explanation as to how, society is to be structured, functional and governed by selected representatives for the common good of man which to some extent, laid the foundation of our modern society that rather unfortunately, is circumvented with numerous complexities of inequality, political intrigues with hilarious Human Rights violations.

The question is what might have gone wrong with the entire social structure that had been put in place, for the benefit and goodness of mankind? in other words, why irrespective of all the pain taking tasks deplored in carving our modern society from the epoch of ancient barbarism and ruthlessness yet, profound traces of vandalism and human anarchy still dominate and threatens our basic values and civilization to a point of extinction? The examination and elucidation of this question could not be a simple one as, it couldn't be referenced to one single academic school idealism but several which upon replication, presented more confused variants and thus squared up in another debilitation.

The more attempts that are made to perfect our human society, the more it becomes complex to achieve the goal because, the level of sincerity and honesty does not usually accompanied our political and socio-economic intention that is been promised. It seems that both the governors and the governed are locked in "spiritual" and "material" warfare, to establish dominance over each other.

The fracas of our human society has made life so uncomfortable and highly volatile to such an unbearable breaking point that has made man to be in constant mental imprisonment not knowing what the purpose of existence is any longer. "He" lived in mental and physical enslavement in which he worked in it, slept in it, walked in it, have children in it, grew up in it, went to shabby school in it, and probably died in it.

Those who survived the self- created abomination and are in position of trust, majority, either associate themselves with the former ideology that had victimised them for self related benefits or become altruistic exponents of the suffering masses which eventually culminate to the formation of either a new political movement or becoming a vibrant opposition leader against existing establishment.

Despite several attempts to perfect the guiding principles of our, democratic liberalism within the context of "The Rule of Law", certain loop-holes and gray areas, still surface which disfigured and disabled the effective working or functionality of the aforesaid structure. The question is, why irrespective of dynamic and charismatic political advocacy for the strengthening of our society on the basis of the Rule of Law yet; ruthlessness, usurpation of fundamental Rights are trampled upon by those who should have been patriotic exponents to uphold its sacred values? The aim of this book project, is to elucidate those factors which are in place that militates against, our fundamental structure that has been advocated for by intellectuals, political and social Activists in the bid to creating an ideal human environment; free from suppression, injustice, unlawful arrest and detention, illegal and unlawful imprisonment without trial before a legally constituted court system, baseless restrictions of expression, of association, of political choice of candidates without victimization and the practical implementation of free and fair election. The road map to unravel the inhuman devastation of fundamental Human Rights, has been an excruciating challenges for liberal intellectuals, political and social Activists and other minded concerned citizens of the liberal Social Media and journalism which often, compromised with illegal arrest, imprisonment, tortured and death.

The voice of the voiceless, are subjected to being voiceless themselves simply due to suppression by state authority through Curfew Order and the promulgation of Emergency Powers to arrest, detained and imprison without trials. A mockery of our liberal democracy at this junction is established and exposed to the gazed of the whole world. What becomes clear which is rather paradoxical is the justification of "trying to clean up the street and society from hooligans and vandals for the peace and security of the state".

Does it mean that those in authority are not applying the Rule of Law? Of course it goes without saying that, application does to some extent have been applicable but, how applicable and effective it has been is the aim of this project to examine and explain areas that has gross neglect and thus need to be rectified under principles and efficacy of the Rule of Law. In order words, to identify certain structures which must be in place for the effectiveness of the implementation of the Rule of Law which is, foundation of our Human Rights that could be of help to students reading for a political science program and law.

Those who may be fortunate to read this book should understand that, materials in this book are researched based and that they should also do some additional material research investigation to enhance their understanding. However, it is my assurance that much needed areas in this book project are simplistically covered for examination and recapitulation exercises.

DEDICATION

It is my profound desire to dedicate this book project to my mother, my wife and children, brothers and sisters including faithful devotees and associate members of the family. It is my ardent desire first and foremost, to recognise our late junior brother whose life was cut –short while his service to the family and mankind was at its' zenith yet, for the more splendid service of the Almighty God. Michael K. Gbow; although you have gone to the greatest beyond which is the final destination for all mankind yet, the love and affections the family had for you and the memory of your excellent deeds will always remain permanent in our hearts and souls till we meet again.

In order of preference, the dedicatees are as follows:

Mrs Lucinda Dassama, mother (Nee Davis)
Mrs Melrose Mator Dassama (Nee Ngobeh) & Children (Lucinda, Admire and Josephine)
Mr George Bobor Dassama
Mr Michael K Gbow(Deceased)
Miss Josephine Kula Dassama (Deceased)
Mrs Nancy James (Nee Dassama)
Mrs Angela W. Jalloh (Nee Gbow)
Mr Mohamed Kposowa (Associate)
Mr Sidiki Koromah (Associate)
Mr Abu Senesie (Associate)
Mr Abu B. Koroma (Associate)

ACKNOWLEDGEMENT

It is not too easy for a man to stand alone against an established system that is, woefully corrupt and addicted to all sorts of vices of a terrible abomination, sabotage, political intrigues, Human Rights abuses, tribal regionalism and ethnic divide culminating into socio-moral economic decline and rottenness to the core unless such a person, has the ordination of divinity.

How easy to say what we are and yet, become the complete opposite of the reality of our action. In the long history of human existence, only few people have stood the test of time, in open defiance against dictatorship, tyranny, and social exclusionism at their own peril.

The path these patriots and global nationalists choose for the freedom of man, shall never go unnoticed and unrewarded because, of the pivotal and axiomatic contributions made in the making of the twenty first century. It is without doubt that, for ours today, theirs' was given yesterday to which we owed much sense of gratitude.

It is therefore, a befitting gratification to acknowledge a man whose academic and professional ability, stood amongst the rest especially during the political and socio-economic debacle of Sierra Leone and became the philanthropic voice of the voiceless. He gingerly and bravely stood for what was right and defended it to the core for the rest of Sierra Leoneans. His legal skills and competence which emanated from the United Kingdom of Great Britain, has always been of an indelible service to the poor and the defenceless in the bid of hammering justice and, fair play to the afflicted.

Nothing has prevented this person irrespective of countless harassments, imprisonment, social stigmatization and destruction of personal assets to halt his march toward a fight for political irredentism and socio-economic emancipation for all citizens and people of Sierra Leone.

In the hour of maximum danger to his life and that of his family, he stood for truth and truth is acknowledged in this presentation which many protagonists might find embarrassing and uncompromising. It is at this time in a much compelling and unbiased manner that, a man who had given and still actively giving so much for mankind, to be appraised.

The curtain of intellectualism interwoven with, professionalism of a true GENTLEMAN, and of humane character be recognised in the person of **Charles Francis Margai; a jurist and leading academic with a reputable political career that is propounded with calm radiant personality befitting, a national hero of which without being verbose, propelled him through democratic consensus to the leadership of the PMDC POLITICAL PARTY, which he courageously established few years ago as, the third indomitable political force in Sierra Leone in pursuance of, Democratic Rebirth within the ambit of the Rule of Law and Human Rights protection.**

In gratitude of his altruistic and humanitarian works affecting the lives of many people in Sierra Leone within his political and legal expertise, an acknowledgement reflecting on such achievement is endorsed because, from whom much is given, much is owed.

CHAPTER ONE

Theoretical Approach to Rule of Law

To be able to fully understand and appreciate what this all important topic in law means, it is vital to briefly traced it histology with regard to the exponents who first, propounded on the idea of what constitute a decent and "civilize society".

Writing around the 4TH Century, Aristotle, in his pensive thinking, was very concerned about the well being of the ordinary common man, in the phase of Monarchical rule which he envisaged to be, vindictive and brutally suppressive against the cardinal ethos of law. In his presentation, he cautioned against the exercise of overbearing laws over the common man without any justification. Man he argued; was born with certain natural rights which must be recognised and protected within the law. Any society which directly or indirectly obliterate this basic fundamental he went on to argue; will not only jeopardise the effectiveness of good governance but, shall create civil unrest and barbarism which will directly undermine the Spirit of Democratic values.

Society which is a complex dynamic structure can only be more useful and habitable if, certain tools are put in place to create a hob of mutuality between the governors and the governed. Since man is rule by law and not by the wisdom of another man, Aristotle went on to say; it is imperative to establish rules and regulations as a bed-rock upon which decency of human existence could be based. This wide ranging approach of man and society, culminate into serious and dynamic debates amongst Politicians and intellectuals who became mindful of the consequences to fallow if negligence and lack of duty of care dominate the landscape of societal existence.

The question is, what shall become of the rest of the ordinary individual if, guidelines are not put in place to serve as Checks and Balances against dictatorship and the obnoxious exercises of arbitrary powers over the governed?

In the long history of human existence, the price of freedom, has been very brutal and diabolic as man struggled against the odds of political and socio-economic enslavement, perpetrated by the elected few trampling on the rest of `us` as victims of circumstances. The writings of Aristotle in the 4TH Century therefore, served as philosophical eye-opener concerning power concentration and the remedy against it. It was therefore not a surprise when some educated and philanthropists began to reason beyond, the thinking of Aristotle commencing the epoch of the 18TH Century thus, establishing a much vibrant and positively charged crusade against tyranny and dictatorship within the whims of political and socio-economic structure of society.

The blueprint on this approach, as espoused by Aristotle, was a clear submission of the fact that, individualism and collectiveness constitute a gigantic stride in creating awareness amongst the governed about Human Rights issue and how best, it could be protected under the law. The question that lingered in the ears of many political and legalistic intellectuals was; how could it be possible to bring this argument of Human Freedom within the ambits of natural law and justice that, every person was born with the same rights and opportunities irrespective of place of origin, colour of skin, race, language, religion, customs and tradition, sexual orientations and values.

The sensational or cardinal aspect of this argument, could be precisely narrowed down to the principle of Duty of Care which is expected of governors over those the pledged to lead and governed a bound of Social Contract between those who are, elected to manage state affairs and other public offices within, the confines of the law of which any breach, could be fatal and woefully undemocratic.

The dream of having a human society that is free of rancour and injustice; and other malaise is but mere abstractive ideology which denied itself, the concurrent and practical reality of what is thus obtainable in our Real World.

Searching for what truly constitute or come about

Human freedom is not located in any way or another self-styled impressionist ideology but that which many legal intellectuals and political social scientists saw as a pragmatic approach. It was therefore not a surprise when some of these exponents began in the 18TH Century to put forward a much more robust and energizing approach to elucidate the Aristotle approach of individual and collectivism approach.

It will be a remised to ignore the Aristotle's approach on the question of Rule of Law because he excavated the idea and thus serves as eye-opener to the reality of our civic responsibilities Vis-a-Vis that of the elected governors. In fact one would not be wrong to epitomize his 4TH Century works as an "Academic Caterpillar", which systematically cleared the path for the establishment of the Human Rights which was officially put into an Act of Parliament in 1988 being enacted in 1989.

The foundation of this great philosopher's approach, to a great extent, opened intellectual debates on the issue of state and people with the aim of creating systemic structure vibrant enough, to uphold the dignity of people irrespective of their, race, language, colour of skin, religion, values, traditional beliefs and above all political affiliations.

Questions arises along the research approaches which examined in microcosm, the functionality of human society on the path of, peaceful co-existence and retribution that the Aristotle's approach/ findings fell short of its target. It is in this area of shortcomings that, needs cogent attention and analysis. What the Aristotle's approach established was a broad based approach to the concept of, **"FREEDOM"** within the scope and convoluted frame work of society and management by the governors over the governed but without, actualizing the specificity of how it could be achieved.

In order words, Aristotle did not tell us, how to achieve the goal of human freedom and what statutory instruments has to be put in place, for the realization and actualization of his grand and marvellous theoretical hypothesis. Thus, it is against this confused backdrop that, political and social scientists began to make an in-road into his research approach in other to, avail themselves with concretised and resourceful information, for clarity of understanding.

Since the door was left wide opened in connection with Aristotle's hypothesis, academics and politicians who were extremely mindful of human freedom, like Montesquieu, a French political philosopher and Albert Venn Dicey, a British academic and constitutional Lawyer became exponents for the application and promotion of, human dignity and freedom within the scope of natural justice based on equality irrespective of, social background, race and ethnicity, religion and cultural ethos, values and held beliefs. What these exponents intend, to amplify was to simplistically examined and explained how the goal of Aristotle could be achieved through constitutional framework. In order words, they made adjustable extensions in their approach by establishing certain explainable principles within constitutional scope, in the bid to achieving the goal of human freedom as discussed in chapter two.

CHAPTER TWO

⟵⟶

Constitutional Approach to Rule of Law

The broad based hypothetical approach adopted by Aristotle, was made more coherent and easily understandable by a French born philosopher and academics, when he and some of his associates, began to copiously examined the constitutionality of other countries like the United Kingdom of Great Britain and by juxtaposition of other countries, came to the unique discovery that, the reason why political upheavals tend to be minimal to the United Kingdom (GREAT BRITAIN), was the institutionalization of governmental structures put in place which serves as Checks and Balances, in the conduct of the affairs of day–to-day running of government.

(1) MONTESQUIEU RULE OF LAW APPROACH.

In his research findings, relative to what had already being established by Aristotle,

Montesquieu was able to discover that, in the British system of parliamentary government the three organs of government which are; the Legislature (Parliament), the Executive (Civil Service) and the

Judiciary (Interpreters of laws made in the Parliament) are functionally separated. In his perception, Montesquieu argued that, the reason why the British system was modelled at best was due to the fact that, those who made the law, do not carry out the law but the executive while the judiciary only interprets the meaning of what the law is. In his analogy he concluded that, this will give rise to checks and Balances to avoid dictatorship and tyranny from emerging. France he went on to say, had no such governmental structures in place to serve as checks to the dictatorial anarchical administration of the monarchy and thus, was responsible for the French Revolution on the 5 May 1789, when the political electorates, decided to take the law into their hands and rampaged the nation and by 14 July 1789, attacked the national prison (The Bastille), that culminated to the demised of Monarchical France giving rise to Republicanism.

Although Montesquieu had a powerful and well established approach to, the principles of separation of powers which became the bed-rock of Democracy yet, his findings fell short of certain basic understanding as to how, the British system works the way he observed it to be. In order words, he failed to realise that, within the British system, there exist cohesion or fusion of power and not separation. In this regard, it is essential to critically examined Montesquieu beyond his understanding of the political working of the British system of government.

a. The three organs of government such as, the Legislature, Executive, and the Judiciary are not separated but rather, fused functionally under the British cabinet system of government

b. The reason for the fusion is that, most members of the Legislature are also members of the Prime Minister's team as cabinet ministers with executive ministerial position thus creating a political marriage between the Legislature and the executive.

c. Seemingly, the Judiciary system which is headed by the Minister of Justice and Antony General is a cabinet minister which, enable him/her to seat in the legislature to defend government legal policy.

d. However, it could be interesting to note that, irrespective of the fusion yet the judicial organ to certain extent maintained some distance between the two organs in the area of interpretation of the law which it does without favour of the legislature or political executive for example, when there was a constitutional crisis as to indicate where sovereignty is located at best parliament and political prerogative, as happened between 2020/2021, it was the judiciary that stepped in to rule against political sovereignty. In this regard, it was clear stated by the court that, the Prime Minister, had no jurisdiction to close parliament because, parliament /legislature, has juridical right to decide when to close its doors and thus establishing the supremacy of parliamentary sovereignty over political sovereignty.

e. Because of the nature of the British system of government, cabinet ministers that head various government ministries/ departments, owed loyalty to their Prime Minister who is "first amongst equals" on the principle of collective responsibility thus, enabling ministers who seats in the legislature, to support and uphold government proposals and policies.

f. Although it is established that, judges do interprets the law as it sees fit within the frame work of the constitution yet, senior appointment within the judiciary, comes from the floor of parliament even though their salaries comes from other source, consolidated funds.

g. Despite the fact that, parliament are designated to making laws, judges do make laws as their interpretative ability of the constitution, may from time to time, inject new phrases to existing laws for the purpose of clarity which constitute by and large, the making of the law.

h. Also, local authorities are mandated by parliament, to make certain adjustments to existing laws in other to, enhance or facilitate policy implementation within their competence and jurisdictions under delegated legislation and by-laws.

i. Although it is said that law making according to the observation of Montesquieu is restricted to parliament, writs and injunctions made by judges that is legally binding tend to, undermine the efficacy and tangibility of such assumption. Basically speaking, writs and injunctions are legal instructions made by judges, to either tentatively put a hold on issues brought in court or, directly request for the implementation of an order such as, warrant of entry/ arrest.

j.   Orders in council is another area that tend to contract the political idea of separation of power which a French philosopher talks about because, it is a special power which the Prime Minister of Great Britain, uses to make emergency law to deal with, emergency situation without the consent of parliament however, such regulation or law, has to be formally approved by the Queen.

(2)   DICEY RULE OF LAW APPROACH

It should be noted that, Montesquieu was not the only exponents in the research project for the protection of human dignity and freedom within the ambits of the law but also, a reputable academic and jurist who, endeavoured to make clarity in the implementation and interpretation of the law within the ambiance of justice and freedom.

Albert Venn Dicey born around 1835 and died in 1922, was one of the leading scholars in constitutional law and a very reputable jurist who believe that, "Man", was born free and therefore must be, protected by the norms of society. He went on to argued that, no man irrespective of their dispositions in terms of education, social status, ethnicity, culture, religion, political affiliation and place of origin, should and must be under the full protection of the law and must be exposed to the Rights and Privileges as dictated by the constitution of the land.

Recapitulating from the academic stand point of his predecessors, Dicey went on to further argue that, any responsible government that practice and observes the ethos of democracy, is deemed to adhere to the cardinal principles of human decency, protection and the leverage of the economic wellbeing of its people. He went on to say that, in the long history of human existence, progress and prosperity of any nation, depends on the positivistic approach of those in power and their relationship with those they governed. Provision of incentives in the educational sector, agricultural sector, science and technology will by and large, make all the difference.

To achieving this objective, Dicey put forward the following factors which must be enshrined in the constitution for the protection of justice and human rights against tyranny, dictatorship and the abuse of human dignity and natural justice. If society is to be safe for human existence he argued, then it must be structured constitutionally to provide the leverage of **freedom and equality before the law.**

Being a constitutional lawyer and jurist, he became more emphatic on the interpretative nature of the law, in the area of crime and arrest. Accordingly, he argued that, every man was born free and therefore, must be treated with dignity and equality before the law. No man irrespective of the nature of the crime/ offence it is said to have been committed must not be, arbitrarily arrested without warrant or refused to be told the purpose of the arrest. In his deliberation, Dicey simply injected the idea of **equality before the law irrespective of skin colour, race, places of origin, religion and tradition, ethnicity, social class status and political affiliation.**

The rules and regulations that governs the nation must be, designed to accommodate, **freedom of speech, movement, association, right of choice of belonging, right to vote and to be voted for under the concept of franchise, right to education and other social amenities like sporting activities and above all the right to peaceful demonstration.**

For the purpose of clarity, Dicey was able to make rational and simplistic explanations as to what in real terms rules and regulations are meant to be, within the ambits of the law. In this regard, it is essential to critically examined those above factors as follows:

1. **Freedom of speech**. According to Dicey, it is illegal and unjust, to arbitrarily prevent people from expressing their mind and feelings toward certain events or situation. In this regard, **press**

freedom should be allowed as a medium of national information and education. The state should and must not interfere into the autonomy of such benevolent service of and to the people. The press and other informative organizations should be given a free hand, to do their job without duress and harassment from the state and other law enforcement agencies of the state such as the judiciary, the police and other secret agencies control by the state. However, Dicey made it objectively clear that, the question of freedom of speech, should and must be engraved with legal and moral responsibility without which, state intervention becomes inevitable at all cost. In his deliberation before parliament, he made it abundantly clear that, in as much as, right to free speech is to be upheld by the constitution, yet, he went on to argue on the balance of probability that, civic responsibility should and must be, stringently be observed and respected so as to avoid national upheavals for the maintenance of peace, law and order. Irresponsible journalism, libel and sedition should absolutely be discouraged in their diary of work. Any attempt to ignore or violet this cardinal instruction will face the full force and penalty of the law as dictated by the constitution of the land. One's right to freedom of speech is not a free hand to insult, molest and debased others without proofs or tangible reasons of doing so. Those found in such act, shall face the full and abrasive force of the law with impunity.

2. **Freedom of movement and association**. It is constitutionally illegal to restrict movement and association of people without tangible justification. The state should give a free hand to its citizens and people, to go about with their daily activities either in business, social entertainment, religious and political. No one or groups of people shall be, victimised because of their movement and association. It is the responsibility of the state to allow its' citizens the right to assemble from place to place in an organised and peacefully co-ordinated fashion. However, the right to free movement does carry civic and constitutional responsibility such as, non violent and incitement to disrupt

national peace and threats to the security of the state. In order words, the right of free movement should not be an excuse, to engage in hooliganism and other forms of barbarism. Those who are guilty of such behaviour or activities will face the full penalty of the law. Although it is the responsibility of the state to allow free movement and association yet, when state security is subject to threats especially from external factors or forces, it becomes mandatory to withhold or suspend such right under special emergency powers, as enshrined in the constitution and which shall be, a prerogative of power to be exercised by the head of state or government under, curfew order. This emergency power to temporally restrict the civic and constitutional right of the people shall be, implemented with flexibility on the basis of time factor. People on the other hand, should have time to be out and time that is scheduled for the streets to be completely vacated.

3. **Right of choice**. In the long history of political evolution along the pattern of democracy, the values and aspirations of its pivotal concern is that of the people which, is deemed to be a political philosophy of **government by the people, for the people and of the people.** Basically speaking, the values as expostulated is simply requesting government under the principle of the rule of law, to allow or grant constitutional right to its citizens the right of choice and belonging. This means, people who are the political electorates, should be allowed to choice whatever political organizations they would like to associate with without being victimized by others,

4. **The exercise of franchise**. In every democratic state, the people should be allowed by law to vote freely, comfortably and without pressure from any antagonistic elements. This right should be guided by the constitution in such a manner so as to, give credence of international value and trust in the electoral machinery of the country. Under this notion, the idea of vote and to be voted for should be the established parameters of the entire process of political franchising. Any state that

excludes or prevent certain class or group of people from exercising such right, constitute a serious breach of the law and stringent violation of human rights. In order words, the electoral system should be none biased politically and should serve only the interest of the country and its people. Those who are employees of the electoral system or commission, should not be nevertheless, ostracised of their franchise or denied their right to vote for any political party of their choice but must not, use such right, to override the system of free and fair election.

5. **Right to education and other social amenities**. It is constitutionally to be, accorded as citizens the right to education and not as a privileged. In order words, citizens should have the right to be educated and the state, must guaranteed such right. Right to education and the use of other social amenities such as sporting facilities, should be a priority of government for its citizens and not a "politically painted" propaganda to decapitate other political opponents in the bid of winning election. Any political party which constitute the government of the day that ignores investments in human capital, violets the basic core of human rights and freedom under the aforesaid rule of law. What should be noted however is that, one's right to education does not mean an abused of the system such as cheating in an examination in the bid to obtaining special assistance in acquiring examination materials prior to the official day of the examination, and other fraudulent activities such as, bribery related grades enhancement for easy university placement and the like.

6. **Right to peaceful demonstration**. One of the principal clauses of democratic society is, the granting of right to citizens for a peaceful demonstration in an attempt, to indicate to establish authorities the level or leverage of discontentment their policies or actions on specific area of concern had been to which, a message of solidarity show of strength, attempt to dispatch, for speedy resolution. This right has to be guided by civic and moral responsibility of which, requisite permission has to be obtained

and approved by the state in which, the aims and objectives of the demonstration is clearly specified. Organizers of such movement, must realised that, the action of their members, will surely be their responsibility and therefore, should be alerted against any act of violence. Any incidence resulting to property damage and injury culminating to death, will be met with a vehement force in the bid to protect lives and properties and to restore, stability and confidence in the state in the "eyes" of international communities. It is usually fashionable to establish accusation that government has being undemocratically over reactive which objectively, tend to be questionable because, it isn't every step that government takes to curb national upheavals, could be undemocratic but rather, constitutionally mandatory to protect citizens and people of the state and to secure international reputation of the national at large.

Over view of Montesquieu and Dicey

The basic understanding of the approach relating to, the rule of law which stem out of the earlier philosophical theory of Aristotle's "society and man", as propounded by Montesquieu and Dicey was that of, functional efficacy of the application of separation of power for the protection and sustainability of decent society and human rights. Accordingly, it is argued that, any break or fracture in the chain of operation of the aforesaid principle, society will be doomed and human rights will be constantly subjected to, dictatorial abuse and anarchy of an unimaginable proportion will overshadowed the decency of society. It is against this backdrop that, a constitutional enforcement of the separation of power should be paramount.

However, it is important to realise that, flexibility and rigidity are opposite to each other and that, what is flexible tend to endure the pressure of time than rigidity. Man and society or vice-se- versa can be effectively functional with flexibility than the later because, it is easier for rigidity to break apart than flexibility.

The interjection of **fusion of power** rather than separation and the codification of constitutional **checks and balances** makes the entire difference. In the **British parliamentary or cabinet system of government**, members of cabinet are chosen from the floor of parliament by the Prime Minister as head of government. These Secretaries as they are usually referred to, head various ministries in the political civil executive thus creating a link to the legislature. Also, the judiciary is linked to the legislature through the minister of Justice who is a member of parliament and one of the senior cabinet appointee of the Prime Minister.

In view of the above synopsis, it is of no doubt that, what is actually obtainable within the ambits of the Montesquieu approach is that of fusion of power rather than total separation because, the three organs of government, are interdependent. In the United States of America, where the system of government is strictly presidential, the notion of power separation is different from Britain because, members of the presidential team or political executive are chosen from outside and not from the floor of Congress. This clearly indicates the difference between the British Cabinet System of government to that of, the presidential type which exist in the United States of America. What should be noted with some aspect of indistinctive clarity is, the convolution of Cabinet System which by political definition is meant to have only one floor of parliament but rather in Britain, the American type of presidential system is devised; House of Common and the House of Lords which by juxtaposition, could be that of the House of Representatives and the Senate under the umbrage of the Congress.

When the academic jurist, AV Dicey approached the argument for the safety of human society, he became profoundly concerned about the preservation of human dignity based on equality before the law. The question is, how truly equal are, we in the phase of the law when society is being classified as "the haves and they have not". Those in higher societal classification like **the rich and the most powerful**, tend to enjoy both the material and spiritual aspects of society than those who are relegated to the dustbin of society. Thus, the term "equality before the law", has to be objectively used so as to do justice to one's conscience of interpretative judgement of the law. The oxymoron that usually surfaced in democratic debates, relates to the emphasis of equality before the law which is not, applicable in real terms in situation where people are arrested without warrant, jailed without fair judicial trials, dispensation of illegal justice against the poor and less economically and politically affluent and those connected to higher places in society. It is absolutely incongruous to suggest that, human rights are stringently protected in the arena of such practical happenings in society. Thus, the question of separation of powers and equality before the law is more dogmatic and therefore, subject to, objectivity and relativity.

CHAPTER THREE

Geo- Political System and
understanding Rule of Law

To simply understand the principles and application of the rule
of law within, western democratic hemisphere and make sweeping
generalization of the effectiveness of the dogma across the entire world,
would be an incalculable error because, political system and machineries,
differ across the geo-political sphere.

It could be a total political disarray to assume that, the practicality
of the principle of the rule of law, as adumbrated in the western
hemisphere, could be functionally the same as that of other countries
in the third world. If countries in the western hemisphere do from
time to time, struggles with the efficacious application of the rule of
law, it could be an anathema to assume otherwise for Socialism and
Communism per-say.

In the far east, the question of the rule of law, is but a myth which
does not really exist but that, which is based on man's most dangerous
imagination which could lead to political, social and economic blackout
that crippled and destroy the goodness and the beauty of humanity and
therefore, must be opposed and stamped out so that, man and society

can be harmonised for peace, happiness, progress and mutuality of understanding.

The proponents of this mythical ideology of the rule of law, argued that, it is not difficult to see as clearly as possible why, those who are practising such societal abomination are always infested with riots, vagrant demonstration, destruction of properties and infrastructures, injuries related death, political unrest and usurpation of power which culminates into economic backwardness disaster. This rather unfortunate situation, give rise to joblessness, poverty, disease and mental instability that further damages any prospective project of government thus resulting into national stagnation and degradation.

It was further argued that, the State should be the mouthpiece of the people and must determine what is best for its' citizens and people and must remain in constant control of events. To delegate responsibility to certain segmented group formation in society in the name of Civil Right Activists is to create "DOOMS DAYS" because, unrest and other social Malaise could be common place since certain irresponsible and malcontents political elements could use such, as an umbrage to destabilize peaceful society and progressive system of government.

In third world countries, the practice of so called "Democracy" is an anathema especially in the application of the rule of law which in most cases result into mere riddle and mockery.

Political unrest, economic decline, despicable social rottenness and a systematic dismantling and destruction of, Human Rights in the name of state security constitute the order of the day. If it is to be a question of debate, as which side of the argument could the conscience of a reasonable outcome, going to be, Should it be neither there or none?

It is most commonly said that, countries that practices democracy, tend to have frequent social and political unrest and economic disruptions than those countries on the other side of the political divide.

It is being assumed that, the effective functionality of the rule of law, is obtainable under **ONE PARTY DICTATORSHIP** than **MULTI PARTY SYSTEM** of liberal democracy due to the fact that, the latter creates social divisions based on ethnicities especially in third world countries that are bedevilled by multiple tribal ethnicities. In this shambolic political frame work, it will be difficult, to distant tribal ethnicity from the structural foundation of emerging political parties that sees themselves as patronage of the dominating tribe of the region it is emanating from.

Illustrating the above assumption, it will be unquestionable to detest in its slightest form, that a political party that is deeply rooted in the **K ZONE** amongst a major tribal group could not claim patronage and homage to such political party. Although other tribal groups could certainly exist within the enclaves of the **K ZONE** yet, their minority denomination, could denied them the overall command and championship of the political party in question.

This political formula could create a politically divided nation on the bases of, regional tribalism and ethnicity. It is thus at this stage that one begin to see, a convoluted politics on tribal and regional platforms appealing to the people's conscience as, to who they are and what the stand for in terms of gain and loss.

Such ideology, could erase all aspects of nationalism where by people could now be seen themselves as exponents and stalwarts of the political party that represents them ethnically.

Could it be fair to say that, under such incongruous political atmosphere, efficacy of the application of the rule of law is obtainable? Members of the political party that happen to have, constituted a government usually would be in the position to manipulate the system in their favour by hijacking the effective implementation of the rule of law especially where members of the ruling party, tend to have been, involved in direct violation of the rule of law.

CHAPTER FOUR

⎯⎯

Understanding and Application of Rule of Law within Communist and Socialist System of Government

In order to fully comprehend the basic philosophies of the two political systems, it is essential to make a juxtaposition of the two so that, clarity of direction of the application of the rule of law could be enhanced for argument sake. What should be note is the synopsis of the two systems rather than, some detail political analysis of the functionality of the two political dogmas. In this regard, this part of the topic will be limited in scope to keep within the framework of this book.

Communism and Socialism, tend to be like "husband and wife" in which, Communism tend to be the political husband while, Socialism tend to be the woman. Paradoxically, these two political ideologies arise from the same political backdrop of, seeking the wellbeing of the people they lead but along the way, a diversion occurs which makes all the difference.

Communism speaks of total state control of economic and production resources for the common good of it citizens in which class division tend to be non existence. In this scenario, equality of it citizens politically, economically, and socially is paramount. In this regard, national wealth or economic resources from production are shared equally with no disparity. Because it tend to advocate for a classless based society in which private owned property is nonexistence therefore, distribution of national wealth is for all according to, ability and needs.

Under such system, what should be the expectant practice of the rule of law? From common sense approach, it should be superb and highly congenial in terms of fair judicial trials conducted in the open with photography and journalistic presence, accursed persons given the opportunity to seek legal representation and be deemed innocent until, proven guilty, unbiased judicial judgement irrespective of who they are and their vocations in society, right of appeal and right to voice grievances in the social media.

In continuity of this proposition, citizens under such system should have freedom of speech, religion, association and right to demonstration against the irregularity of state and government performances. Paradoxically, upon close examination, this assumption tend to be a myth which baffled common sense approach in the epoch of modernism and postmodernism because, a political system which vouch to protect and preserve the lives, interest and dignity of its people, should and most be committed to safeguarding and upholding the principles of Human Rights and not the other way.

Historical account of past and current happenings, have glaringly, brought to the attention of the world how countries that does practiced such political philosophy and ideology, have been ruthlessly heavy handed on their citizens who attempt to test their alienable human rights under the law. The question is; should it be possible to have a system that lent itself on the political platform of seeking the total interest of its people in the "morning" and yet in the "evening", a total monster? Should Socialism which is closely related to Communism be exceptional to this paradox? To some extent, this system which slightly deviates from its original format could be much more acclaimed to, reasonably observing Human Rights within the political spectrum of the rule of law.

Since Socialism tend to cater for the needs of its citizens in which, it pledges total and equal distribution of resources and economical production on the basis of needs and ability, it means that, those who are potentially contributing to the economic process of production, enjoys its blessings spiritually and materially through private ownership of properties. This further means that, to some extent in juxtaposition of Communism, the observation of Human Rights under the application of the rule of law tend to be more secured than under Communism.

However, it is essential to note with dismay that, even where Socialism tend to do at best, it equally creates a political stamped which absolutely evaporates its good nature and flavour of governance due to, bulling political tactics to silence the fundamental principles of Human Right s and the misguided interpretation of, the rule of law for the benefit of the ruling class and elites.

No matter which way the "coin" of game is flinched into the air and back to the ground, it reads a caution of malapropism in the grounding of the usage of the phrase, **Rule of Law** because it doesn't level to its expectation of efficacy for all and sundry.

CHAPTER FIVE

Understanding the Application of Rule of Law within Democratic System of Government

It is without any doubt to say that, a Democratic system of government, does the magical tricks of what the Rule of Law stands for in principles and as well as in application because it tend, to strongly advocate and adjudicate for it as the pivotal political nervous system of any decent and purely representative government which is ; elected by the people on the basis of choice free of intimidation, harassment, vote rigging, marginalization of political constituencies, tribal and regional sentiment, right of the people, by the people and of the people which geared to the protectionism of Human Rights as enshrined in the Human Right s Act of 1988.

Basically, any Democratic Constitution around the world at large could be exponential in delivering and protecting, the fundamental principles of Human Rights within the ambits of the Rule of Law. Over the centuries, questions have been raised as to how far this challenged responsibility, have been achieved. In order words, how Democratic are the institutions of governments, by the people on the basis of choice free of rancour be truly achieved in the phase of awkward happenings around the world where especially, these Democratic institutions are established.

It seems absolutely ironically to talk of the efficacy of Democratic principles and values in countries which are well established on the political platform of "Democratic ideology", to have bumpy ride in administration through suppressed tactics and open violation of the principal values on which it was founded. The aftermath of economic mismanagement which does creates artificial poverty, social maladjustment, class distinctions between the very rich and the very poor, injustice and unlawful imprisonment without trial, the deliberate destruction of the media and other means of communication, political tension due to vote rigging and unlawful arrest and imprisonment of opposition leaders and above all, the systematic killing of members of opposition parties thus creating a situation where the principles of the Rule of Law, becomes a mirage in real terms by application which is a riddle in the fulfilment of what Democratic values truly are.

To speak of Democratic values in countries where, its political foundation was laid and propagated throughout the global hemisphere as requisite is "accidental" in terms of its opposite nature, a myth to common sense application and judgement. It is a mere riddle which by and large, creates a terrible misconception of the phrase; "Democratic values and principle". It is without any doubt that, the backdrop of any Democratization should literally correspond to a set of human and societal values for the cordiality of peace, development, human dignity of purpose, fair justice and equality before the law, protection and the maintenance of good government based on choice, the bridging of class for economic sustainability and political stability.

Over the centuries, it is being recorded and observed with horror the sabotage of Democratic principles and values, especially in countries that preaches the political "gospel" of its machinery. It has now become, a mere rubber stamped ideology which is often used by the ruling class to gain political height and become like a massive colossus which bestride the narrow passage for the common man to pass through for humiliating existence.

It is of no doubt to say that, countries that has its political ideology based on the principles of Democratic values, are usually predisposed to social malaise and electoral malpractices especially where, the ruling party or the party in power is struggling to regain its political power and status in a multiparty based election which, it feels threatened with a possibility of defeat.

Conversely, those opposition parties could likely engineer unrest and other related sabotages such as, organised demonstrations which usually end violently with serious repercussion relating to the destruction of private and government properties, infrastructures and lives. The "seeds" of hatred and vagrant ill-feelings towards each other, damages the economy and poisoned bi-lateral and international relationship of the country and create an atmosphere of uncertainty, mistrust and other distasteful portrayer affecting international trade and global political friendship.

A glaring evidence of perpetual political struggles and violence in which, each political party or organizations, engaged each other could be without saying that, micro-economic damages affecting standards of living culminating into poverty related starvation, poor health, unsanitary existence, increased level in prostitution, increased level in abortion and death, single parenting, child abuse and molestation with little or no effort by the state to addressing the situation which tend to escalate daily until it becomes a way of life which people have to put up with or remised.

The question which rational thinkers, have been puzzled about is, why irrespective of all the necessary structures in place especially, in third world countries (Africa); structures such as the institutions of law enforcement, law making and interpretation of judicial system, and a well organised political system which is recognisable by world body of world government (UNO) and the like yet, so much democratic failings, have always bedevilled Africa and other third world countries the most.

In order words, why despite third world countries especially Africa, having a standardised Democratic mechanism that could be similar to developed and advanced countries in the western hemisphere yet, a vagrant and brute force dominate the political and socio-economic "skyline" of Democratic practice?

Have we been able to trace or locate the reasons why this is or have been the case or happening the way it is happening?

Is there any systematic correlation in third world Democratic practice to that of the western hemisphere? In most of the researches that have been undertaken by social scientists and political thinkers, a caution unanimously have been put across which most likely could not be ignored irrespective of its ugliness at best. In this regard, it is but absolutely essential to make a synoptic visitation of the **Accident of Colonial Hegemony and Colonial Past** in an attempt to unravelled the present day mystery of Democratic setback and mess as it is in modern times especially in Africa.

What came to be a uniform structured within a Democratic aspiration, is rather the opposite because, its exponents did not realise or maybe, deliberately ignored the fundamental values of the colonised people in terms of cultural identities, values, tradition and customs, religion, ethnicities and tribal regional demarcations as factors to have been stringently considered before, the institutionalization of Democratic political values on their colonies. What is being observed over the centuries is that, the importation of this strange and unusual political practice which the colonisers transplanted into the political system of Africa, without caution has by and large, fragmented whatever good intentions they have had.

To practise a system which is exotic without any modernization or adjustment is fruitless and could be caustically dangerous because, it may backfired. Over the years, Africa politicians have had a rigorous task of making western oriented Democratic principles work as "effectively" as it does in theirs yet, the result had always been dismal due to regional and tribal conflicts upon which the entire political system tend to revolve.

If one takes a mental journey into the western hemisphere, what could be realised is the absence of a visible tribal groupings especially in Britain, France, Germany, United States of America Italy to name but few.

It is of no doubt therefore that, Democratic values of multi party system and the rule of law, to some extent tend to be more secured and adhered to when it comes to the interpretation and implementation of the rule of law than, it does in Africa and other third world countries. It is but necessary to examined as to why, this is the case in Africa and other third world countries at large. In this regard, the principle of Correlative Approach will be examined within the context of applicability in conjunction with, values, tradition, culture, belief system tribal and regional demarcations and other social ethos. The reason for this is that, it could be morally dangerous for strange or foreign ideology to be, transfused into another global community without first and for most, not rigorously embarking on "Assimilation Process" in the bid to helping nativity to grab the essentials and thereby, creating a corridor of mutual understanding as to how such ideology, could be practiced along traditional valued system to avoid clash and other forms of diabolism.

It was not difficult to reason with some of the African educated elites especially in the French Colonial territories like Senegal, Mali, Ivory Cost and Guinea Conakry to name but few, where the French Colonial Administrators, applied the policy of Direct Rule ended up in a terrible political fiasco because, the early African Nationalists, began to question the validity and applicability of the French Colonial policy of Direct Rule from the "**MOTHER COUNTRY-FRANCE**", on the basis of **ASSIMILATION** into French Black citizenship programme.

The question that was on Nationalist lips was why should Black people be subjected to a foreign policy which had no relevance in the Africans ways of life?

It was not a surprise to realised that, those nationalists where able under great political constraints and victimizations, to form the first political opposition party against the French Policy of Assimilation abbreviated and interpreted as **R D A** (Any political Ideology Must Resembled Democratic Values of the African People) which means, all forms of political ideologies from France must be characterised wit African values and capable of recognising and accommodating Africa traditional ways of life and social ethos.

What those freedom fighters and nationalists saw and rose against their Colonial administrators was based on the fact that, Western style Democracy, was going to be absolutely problematic unless it reflects on the African values. It is rather unfortunate to note over the years that, the philosophical ideology behind the **R D A** was not pursued vigorously by modern days nationalists and thus, responsible for major political upheavals in the continent as to day.

The question is what went wrong? Although several attempts have been made by most educated Africans to answer the above question yet, no one had successfully addressed the pivotal issue for the demised of the aspirations of **R D A** because, of differences that existed in the geo- regional colonial political patterns of administration within **FRANCOPHONE** and **ANGLOPHONE** colonial hegemony.

It couldn't therefore be surprising to conclude one of the reasons as to have been closely related to, mutual trust and understanding amongst, the political elites and nationalist freedom fighters who unfortunately, where fighting on the same colonial administrative platform but with different political interpretative ideology.

Those within the French territories arguably saw the policy of Assimilation of a Democratic nature, as a direct citizenship opportunity to the mother country France and thus, providing equal privileges to the black Africans that had fulfilled the criteria of citizenship by being educated and speaking the French language with French accent, dressing like French men and women, and adopting French mannerism. This was some of the benevolent offer which, the exponents of **R D A** philosophy, couldn't afford to resist because, it offers them a silent political platform of leadership in which, they will be opportune to handle the political and socio- economic affairs of their countries as "French Black Politicians" following the exit of white French colonial administrators.

The Anglophone nationalists and freedom fighters saw the black political Francophone as paying a lip service to the struggle of Africa total Liberation movement by, subjugating their respective countries to France in terms of direct taxation, exportation of raw materials, importation of finished products only from France and the conduction of political election by the supervision of only France. It was also observed that, the issue of French Citizenship and Subject ran simultaneously in the territories in which, irrespective of political independence, the Blacks were still not able to enjoyed the freedom which they had dreamt of, because those who were not able to master the French language and culture and thus classified as "French Subjects", had little or no protection under the French Worded Constitution in terms of being arrested and jailed without trials and most often, ended up serving longer prison sentences.

With a clash in political ideology, the union of black Nationalists movements began to crack and setbacks became inevitable.

Conversely, the Anglophone nationalists, saw the system of indirect rule through the Native Institutions of Paramount chiefs, as a total humiliation by the educated elites who at that time felt that, their right to leadership, was been forcibly taken from them, and given to illiterate paramount chiefs, who would be of no constructive use in the making of the affairs of their respective countries but rather been subservient to the will and aspirations of the English colonial administrators. This master- servant relationship, was frowned upon by the Black Francophone Nationalists and Freedom Fighters who saw a total reject of the educated Blacks in the English hegemony and therefore, must not be associated with because, it was by their description, "A **vermin and dangerous political insects**" that has to be avoided at all possible cost.

It was not surprising to note with dismay, a differential rift in the ranks and files of the early black nationalists freedom fighters of Africa. This aspects of their political and socio-ideological differences especially between the **CASABLANCA AND THE MONROVIA GROUP OF PROTERGONISTS**, created a huge and monstrous barrier in the arena of, regional cooperation which was a situation that bedevilled the establishment of the ever first inter-regional federation of the **United States of Africa** as was intended.

Had this gap of ideological differences harmoniously be compromised and unified, African leaders and political enthusiast, would have been able, to device political mechanisms whereby, western Democratic ideology could have been inculcated into the African political system based on cultural and traditional values of the continent. In order words, the western Democracy could have been practiced along Africa systemic values, culture, tradition, tribal settings and demarcations.

In the absence of all of the above, it is rather a very sad reality to note that, the western Democratic ideology which was imported into the continent of Africa, being practiced along same, have had a prolonged bitterness of disasters which is a situation the continent is struggling with.

The question which one could be tempted to look at is; what goodness or progressiveness has this ideology brought to the continent? In other words, has it been of a unified force under its umbrage the continent has seen and witnessed peace, tranquillity, stability, social harmonization, economic development and equitable justice.

In the summation of this chapter, without any form of prejudice rather on the balance of probabilities, the Rule of Law which is embedded within the political internal structure of Democratic principles has not been effectively user- friendly and thus, little or zero efficacy rating in Africa. **NOTE: It was only Guinea-Conakry which systemically stood against the French hegemony and denounced it as Despotic Colonialism under the leadership of Sheku Turay.**

CHAPTER SIX

Merits and Demerits of the application of Rule of Law within Communism and Democratic Capitalism

This part of the discussion is not about Capitalism versus Communism in terms of, which is best and which is appalling both rather, a juxtaposition of material facts along which these two political philosophical ideologies, have wallowed its way through the mind set of people in the bid, to creating a perfect and decent human society which could be free of all forms of defects for excellent existence of the human race. The question to be addressed is; how effective has this two philosophies been of positive influence in our society and people.

It is without any shred of doubt that, the impact of these two ideologies have, deeper geo-political divide in human physical environments and in our mind-set in terms of, perception and reaction of our daily activities.

The creation of symbolic emblems such as flags bearing banners, slogans, national anthems, membership identification codes and specific colour bearing that depict one's membership and sense of belonging, all constitute the meaning of who we are and what we literally stand for. Nationalism and nationalist movement all have inextricable linked to national symbolisms on which national identities are exemplified at best.

The national's flag and emblems are sufficient justification as to what it stands for in terms of either being Communist, Socialist or Democratic institution. For example, when one sees the Chinese red flag with couple of stars in scripted, Communist perception is arose within us and as a result, the question of the Rule of Law in terms of how it is been practice becomes an dubious as our suspicion of Human Rights violation, takes the central stage of our though.

Conversely, an American Flag with its red strips couple of stars against a white background, the British Flag, the German flag, Italian flag, the French flag and Sierra Leonean flag, our perception of Democratic institution is triggered within which, the Rule of Law is supposed to be judiciously practiced and observed in conformity with Human Rights observation and protection.

Our perceptions of flags and colour codes, to a great extent influenced our ways of life and behaviour. During a football match, fans are seen dressed and gingerly walked into the sporting arena, singing and waving their respective flags and other emblems that identified them to each participating team; in which they are usually seen fight in it, maliciously damage properties in it and even killed each other in it.

A man who dressed up in Chinese Communist flag attired and, stands on Broadway New York preaching about the good life China offers to the world, could be immediately apprehended for questioning by the F B I and other secret services, for state protection. It is really paradoxical for symbolic imageries, to take the better part of our human intelligence and wisdom and, direct the path of action that follows.

It is usually common sense application that, image and reality could not necessarily be true or the same because, of what shall be revealed upon further investigation. Symbolic imageries could be deceptive in that, it does to some marginal extent, concealed reality and project falsity a notion upon which, our human action becomes eminent simply because, our human brains have been addicted and adaptive to the background of symbolic imageries.

It has now become fashionable especially in political arena for, a person to be easily arrested, charged and even denigrated to prison simply because of her/his loyalty to the symbolic imagery of the political organization that represents his or her interest.

It is common saying that, those who are fortunate to have control of the seats of national government, stands a much far better chance in every aspects of life than those who are not. They are usually for example; considered for better paid jobs irrespective of qualifications, experience, personality, communicative skills and general exposition in life. If the Rule of Law is to protect against, dictatorship, tyranny and the injection of inequality in society before the law, why then, certain class of people tend to rise above its pivotal functions? In order words, why should people be given special treatments and reverence under the law which shouldn't rationally speaking, have been the case.

It is very despicable to note that, irrespective of political ideologies, favouritism is all over the place for party loyalists and exponents as against the ordinary common man which by and large; denigrated the Rule of Law that couldn't have meant to be.

It is therefore, an open secret to realise that, the applicability and functionality of the Rule of Law, to some extent, exist as mere shadows or mirage when confronted with symbolic imagery connection to existing national governments; either in Monarchical structures, Republican Democratic structures, Socialist structures and Communist structures to name but few.

Merits and demerits of the application of the Rule of law at different levels of political philosophical structures of government tend to shift at interval with, little or no regard for consequences to come. The Communists does it, the Democratic Capitalists also embarked upon it as well and at will.

It is difficult to say with precision which, ideology tend to be the best over another when, it comes to the application and delineation of the Rule of Law because of inherent flaws which connects to morality and sense of belonging.

Navigating through this political and philosophical jungle, there are certain ethical questions that has to be addressed such as; which political ideology does best and which one does poorly and finally how does the best by our sense of judgement, be an instrument to make better the one that is poorly structured when upon closed and microscopic examination and observation, the so called "the best", has dirty background.

It is not by own wisdom that society is conducted along the path of justice and fair play but rather, by the dictates of law which men and women of matured wisdom put together which is, vigorously debated upon for clarity and sanctity of purpose.

It is usually possible for contradictions to occur in the application and delimitation of the law which is part of our human frailty base on; loyal and connection yet, where a strong sense of judgement is set in motion, such could be overcome.

Interpretation of the law on literary basis is, indicative of what the law is with regards specific issue at hand which ought to have been where it is deemed necessary by application.

If by application of the law with regards specific act is not inconformity of what it should be or ought to have been then, it takes to question what went wrong and how it could be immediately addressed to avoid constitutional crisis or legal upheaval.

What in most cases have been happening is interpretation of the "law" within the ambits and pleasure of the authorities which had emanated since the time of Colonial rule or foreign hegemony especially in Africa.

During foreign rule in Africa as an illustrated example, the law as it was, deemed to have existed for the comfort and administrative eased of the authority in pursuit of their administrative duties as dictated to them by their superiors from whence they came. In order words, the interpretation of the law was done in such a cleaver way that, tend to always protects and, maintained existing administration at that time than to fairly and judiciously appraise the law for the common good.

The law in simplistic terms was, a backup "mechanical digger" which was politically intended to keep the Colonial Rule in place at all times irrespective of its adverse effects on the people. The question of Human Rights Abuse, was non considerate and in most cases, its exponents were arrested flogged, brutalised and jailed without trials. Those who became humane and advocate for free and fair interpretation of the law as it should be or ought to have been, became the unquestionable enemies of the administrators of the state to which they too, were targeted and brutally victimised. It is rather resentful to have this sort of paradoxical interjection in political Democracy which speaks of a better world for all and sundry.

Since it is complex to deal with, the issues of merits and demerits of the application of the rule of law within the political spectrum of Communism and Democratic Capitalism in paraphrase of essay style of writing, it is essence to analytically discussed the topical subject in question through specific topical headings for purpose of clarity and recapitulation exercise as follows:

1. **The pivotal theme of Communist manifesto**. It was usually the main idea of the exponents of Communist political philosophy to create a society of equals where, no one person(s), could emerged to be more powerful and influential than the rest of others so as to avoid dictatorship and anarchy which could lead to human rights suppression. It was also going to be a system where resources are evenly distributed on the basis of family size and structures with no one emerging to be more powerful, richer, classic, superior and above all, deific.

2. **Equal political representation** irrespective of size of tribe and territorial regions and the protection of all and sundry under the law.

3. **Application of the law** to suit every citizens on the basis of free and open representative trials of all accused persons who will be deemed innocent until proven guilty, by a legally constituted court of jurisdiction.

4. **The creation of free and just society** which allows, freedom of people's movement and right of assembly and right to feely expressed feelings of opinions.

What should be observed in all these pivotal clauses is the applicability of it. It sounds so powerful and absolutely melodious yet, looks like a very powerful drum but without any "band sticks". It is thus highly deceitful to accept on surface value that, Communism does practice the best politics in consonant to the protection and safe guards of the Human Rights liberties.

It is proven beyond all doubts that, Human Rights abuses are more prevalent in countries with Communist political ideology which by and large, denounces its own pivotal manifesto in all aspects of life. The records of Human Rights denial and betrayal are very alarming. The very society it pledges to protects, have been under constant attacks by the police and army in the bid to silent the very people it professes to protect against tyranny and systemic oppression.

The constancy of peaceful administration in Communist system of government as adumbrated in the People's Republic of China, is not truly an efficacy in the application of the Rule of Law BUT RATHER PARTHODIXACALLY, a suppressive mechanism which is set in motion that serves as CHECKS AND BALANCES, not for the purpose of upholding the dignity and integrity of the Rule of Law but to ripped apart every vestiges of what constitutes democratic values and decency such as free speech, movement, assembly, equal representation before the law, fair trials and assumption of innocence before trial and sentencing.

Although the society could be apparently seen to be orderly and peaceful where, everything seems to be going in the right direction yet, when examined in microcosm, a larger picture of discontentment will emerged but which the oppressed people are unable to do nothing about. In this regard, based on objectivism, it could be established that, what one sees as an orderly and peaceful society because of the application of the Rule of Law, is an absolute fraud and betrayal of Democratic values which could not be visible without explicit examination.

Thus in conclusion, when an examination of Communist system is objectively analysed, the application of the Rule of Law could be seen as a political instruments in the hands and control of government, to always maintain the peacefulness of the streets, media reporting, and movement of its people but which, is in actuality against the people who are silent to death by the state oppressive apparatus thus making the efficacy of the Rule of Law void.

Conversely, when an objective examination of a Democratic system of government is juxtaposed with Communism, a glaring difference is what is in the open in Democracy by allowing expression of views or opinions, assemblies, demonstrations, medial expressions, open court hearing procedures which culminate into "fair trials", and the establishment of opposition political parties yet, it constitute the same as in Communism because, despite its openness it is relative of the fact that, favouritism, nepotism, party loyalty and the inordinate desire to maintained power at all cost especially in third world Democratic states, that tend to operate on pretentious policy of open Democracy but with vindictive machinery in place to sustained their power based at the detriment of the people. In this regard, one could safely argue that, the Rule of Law in both systems are at level crossing with each other in which one tend to be, opened and the other closed thus making or rendering the efficacy doctrine of the Rule of Law opaque and dubious.

CHAPTER SEVEN

The inter-play of Philosophy and Psychological Approaches of Rule of Law

It has never been a topical area of academic and political discussion because of either, due to its sensitivity or the embarrassment it could have created if, such had been, an area of academic or political discus. It is difficult to always skip the truth of life and pretend it does not matter or exist of which knowingly, such truth rely do exist with perpetual effects on our daily activities if an endeavour is attempted to unearth the truth of our social being. The question that could be put across is; why certain things happened the way it does and why, no attempt has been made to follow its intricate pathway in the bid to find out the answer. It is being proven beyond all reasonable doubts that, mysticism could be a direct result of the failings of man's inability to take a giant step forward on a fact finding mission. Those brave academics, anthropologists, political analysts, scientists, biologists, legal expertise and geographers to name but few, have had their names and discoveries of the unknown in the making of our pre-modern and modernism of our human world as it is today.

The topic under discussion is a direct challenge to what is being happening to our society and, the adverse effects, on our psychological well-being and makeup which rather unfortunately, had either being ignored due to ignorance or, deliberately ignored to avoid social upheavals to the peril of man.

Philosophy and psychology do play an awesome role in our human society because, these two provides platforms on which, everyday happening tend to occur with mixed result and apprehensions.

Philosophy tend to broaden our human mental thinking by, series of tantalising material knowledge and theoretical based suppositions that, unquestionably affects the way we think and behaved without at times, objectivism due to the indelible material impacts on our brains for total subservient belief of material "facts" for subjectivism. It is crystal clear a saying that; "habits once inculcated or learnt unquestionable for protraction of time, becomes biblical facts even where there is room sufficient to question its validity".

This therefore becomes very dangerous because, it damages our psychological thinking and subjected us to all sorts of vices to the peril of society and our social relations. Those who may be in political positions, to determine the faith and destiny of society could simply used these established philosophical dogmas, to hold society against the rest to maintain power at all cost.

Illustratively speaking, it could be realised that, whatsoever is being practiced in our modern society is that which had been inculcated into us through dogmatic philosophy which at times, we refer to as traditional and customs in which our existence is being modelled at best.

The danger or damaging effects these philosophical teachings that impinges on our psychical makeup does to our intelligence, goes extra miles to determine who we are and what we do stand for. It is common place to establish rational re-think that, most of our human actions or activities, are or have been influenced by, dogmatic philosophy that at times makes us to be controlled by unavoidable instincts.

It may sound or appeared to be absurd against the backdrop that, "man" being an intelligent existent, has the power of "will" to by and large, determine his own, pathway in life by matter of choice which is dictated by objectivism and subjectivism. In this regard, it is a fundamental truth to be established that, in our own hands and domain lies, the machinery of both destruction and rectification of ambiance for the common good and ugly of us all.

What has to be noted is that, every philosophical teachings or doctrines, makes direct appeal to our conscience in the bid of establishing "new facts/ideology" upon which, our behaviour and actions are modelled at best. If it is to be questioned as to what extent does, our ability to interrelate with our indoctrinated philosophy could be referred as best, which of the "best" could it be? Is it the "best" for our selfish gratification to the detriment of the rest of society or, is it that "best" which rationally dig into reality and come up with positivistic solutions for the common good of society?

To be simplistically illustrative, it is essential to discuss the above approach into subsections as follows:

1. **Application of indoctrinated philosophy only for the self**: it a natural occurrence in man to develop interest in what is being learnt only for the benefit and, usefulness that pleases his desire to remain at the top of the rest of society irrespective of diabolic cost. If a dictator uses the Principles of the Rule of Law, it could be at his advantage in arguing that, "law and order has to be maintained for the protection and safety of society," in this regard, those who legally demonstrate against the abuse of the law, will unquestionably be arrested, flogged brutally, imprisoned without trials and in most cases tortured to death like beasts. It is absolutely illusive to note when, juxtaposition is illustrated between a dictatorial authority applying the Rule of Law and that of the exponents of the general masses (Human Rights Activists). While those dictators will be applying illegal justification, the Human Rights Activists looks at the abused of the Rule of Law which unfortunately, brings further punishments to them to which there can be no redress for justice in a court of law.

2. **Application of indoctrinated Philosophy only for the common good**. This is the opposite of what is being discussed above. It is applicable for the good and decency of human societal existence. It concerns itself with, the achievement of a smooth and progressive society of equal representation before the law irrespective of, race, creeds, religion, values, customs and places of origin. In this regard, those in authority, only apply the law as dictated by the courts on the basis of independent judicial judgement which could be biased free. In this supposition, those who violate the law are punished according to, the dictates and leverage of the law as interpreted by a legally constituted court of the land, functioning on the basis of free hands devoid of political interference.

Based on what is being discussed, it could be interesting to note that, what comes into our human brains is very delicate because, it determines the way we behaved in terms of perceptions which could either be negative or positive. It conversely makes us to perceive others as inferior and treat them diabolically and with rotten stigma while, positioning ourselves as superior race and conqueror of all existence.

The philosophical indoctrination of the principles of the rule of law which, dictators applied in giving circumstances could be ironical for the simple fact that, it does not truly and honestly, reflects on the common good but rather, on the fulfilment of brutality against the very people it pledges to protect.

Most often, dictators have been applying principles of "legality" to perpetrate act of violence in the bid to erased or stamped out all forms of political agitators and protagonists that could be a threat to their regime as well as making annexation under the pretext of "territorial right of ownership"

Thus in this scenario, it could be assumed that, the application of the rule of law, thus has some profound degree of ramification which could not be simply deduce to legality of the law as stipulated by Acts of Parliament but rather, by the dictates of instincts deemed fit by authorities at that material time in question.

It is becoming a mere fun of intellectual game to suppose that, Acts of Parliament which intentionally stipulates, moral and legal guidelines as to how best, man and society could co-exist peacefully, has been a mere shadow with no effective related outcome in most cases.

CHAPTER EIGHT

Conclusion

The ease of society depends on, the degree of honesty and fervent dealings that operates within its structural frame work. If for any reason a shift occurs, it will shake the very foundation of decency, security, trust, freedom and justice which by every moral standards, ought to have been entrenched.

Man made rules and regulations which rather unfortunately, made us subservient to the very rules and regulations put in place. In order words, what man puts together initially in the bid to create suitable and worthy society for all, will be a test case of her/his, inner ability to fulfil them which most often than none, depicts the inner sincerity of us all.

The applicability of the rule of law is a moral reflection of, who we are and what we stand for in our society and how, reflective the badge of sincerity we professed to have. What is being put together by man in an attempt to make life comfortable and fruitfully progressive, can only be meaningfully achieved provided, our "hand are clean" or else, mockery of failure will as it is, and seemingly in the years to come.

To assume the best for our human society is a mere mirage due to, the limitation and imperfection that characterises our creation. It is absolutely contradictory in purporting that, "we" posse it all because, the human society is never perfect.

Therefore whatever, is inculcated to make a beautiful blend of perfection of "sinful earth", is an anathema which is wrapped up in the bud of truth which is yet to be discovered.

Nevertheless, it is unfair to surmise that, much has not been done to make our human world an ideal place of peace to live. Irrespective of our gross limitation, human society has been very successful in putting workable structures in place, especially in the 21 Century.

It is absolutely these structures that have propelled our human world to a height of solace, freedom, and the dignity of man above all creations on planet earth.

The Rule of Law is the bed-rock of our democratic values which has to be, protected against adverse abuse and tyrannical dictatorship. To be able to achieve this to the level of efficacy, those who are required by law, to conduct the functionality of the Rule of Law, must do so with "clean hands".

BIBLIOGRAPHY

1. Lowndes and Rudolf et al---Law of general average(2018)
2. Tom Bingham- Rule of Law(2012)
3. Rubin Griffith et al---Magna Carta, Religion, Rule of Law(2015)
4. Kenneth JUPP--- Rule of Law and other essays(2005)
5. Dr Michael Dassama---A Dialectic Approach to Criminal Law(2020)
6. Fernanda Pirie---- The Rules of LAWS(2021)
7. Christopher May-The Rule of Law, Common Sense of Global Politics(2014)
8. Jack Beatson---The Rule of Law and the Separation of Power(2021)
9. Adam Przeworski et al ---Democracy and the Rule of Law(2003)

END.

www.ingramcontent.com/pod-product-compliance
Lightning Source LLC
Chambersburg PA
CBHW021511210526
45463CB00002B/979